FEELING GOOD

DAVID D. BURNS, M.D., was graduated magna cum laude from Amherst College, received his M.D. from Stanford University and completed his psychiatric training at the University of Pennsylvania. There he has been one of the prime developers of Cognitive Therapy. In addition to treating patients, he teaches psychotherapy and drug therapy at the University of Pennsylvania and lectures to professional groups around the world.

Dr. Burns has condensed years of research conducted at the University of Pennsylvania on the causes and treatments of depression for those who wish to give themselves a "top flight" education in understanding and mastering their moods. He presents, in simple language, innovative and effective methods for altering painful depressed moods and reducing debilitating anxiety. FEELING GOOD should prove to be an immensely useful step-by-step guide for people who wish to help themselves.

From the _Preface_